CONTENTS

WHAT YOU NEED

The crafts in this book use materials that you can find in art shops, stationers and around your home. This page shows you the materials you will need to make lots of craft ideas.

Glue stick

Pencils

Paints and paintbrush

Marker pens

Scissors

Coloured paper

Ruler

Assorted pebbles and shells

PVA glue

Follow the simple step-by-step guides to create these wonderful results! Find out how to make scary monsters, dragonflies, ballerinas and much more.

LET'S GET STARTED!

PHILIP
the fish

Gulp!

1 Paint your pebble white. Leave to dry.

2 Sketch your fish design onto the pebble.

TRY OUT ALL THESE DIFFERENT DESIGNS

PEBBLE
ARTY Crafty

WITH SIMPLE STEP-BY-STEP INSTRUCTIONS

MARK BERGIN

Published in Great Britain in MMXIX by
Scribblers, an imprint of
The Salariya Book Company Ltd
25 Marlborough Place,
Brighton BN1 1UB
www.salariya.com

SALARIYA
SCRIBO BOOK HOUSE SCRIBBLERS

© The Salariya Book Company Ltd MMXIX

ISBN-13: 978-1-912537-41-9

1 3 5 7 9 8 6 4 2

A CIP catalogue record for this book
is available from the British Library.

Printed and bound in China.

Printed on paper from sustainable sources.

Visit
www.salariya.com
for our online catalogue and
free fun stuff.

3 Paint in the body colour of the fish.

4 Then paint in the main design. Leave to dry.

5 Add all final details to complete.

SCARY monsters

1 Paint a pebble white. Leave to dry.

2 Now paint it blue, leaving the eyes white.

3 Once dry, paint in the black eye pupils.

4 Add a mouth and paint in teeth.

5 Try out an assortment of different eyes, mouths and teeth.

9

CHRISTOPHER
the crab

clack

clack

clack

1 Paint a flat oval pebble red. Leave to dry.

2 Now paint in two white eyes.

3 Paint in black eye pupils and the mouth.

4 Place your pebble on a piece of red card and draw around it.

5 Now draw in the crab's claws and legs.

6 Use scissors to carefully cut out the shape of your crab.

7 Stick the pebble crab to the card using PVA glue.

clack

clack

clack

11

PATRICK
the pirate

Shiver me timbers!

1 Paint your pebble white. Leave to dry.

2 Paint in the face. Leave the top white.

3 Once dry, paint in the bandana.

4 Draw in the nose and paint it.

5 Draw and paint the eyes and mouth using black and white paint.

6 Make the bandana stripy. Add teeth and scars!

yaaargh!

TRY MAKING MORE FEARSOME PIRATES!

SIMON the snowman and PETE the penguin

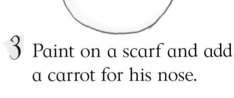

1 Choose a long pebble to paint white. Leave to dry.

2 Paint in black dots for the eyes, mouth and buttons.

3 Paint on a scarf and add a carrot for his nose.

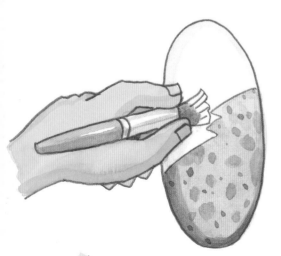

1 Choose a long pebble to paint white. Leave to dry.

2 Pencil in the shapes (as shown) and paint the rest in black.

3 Now paint in an orange beak and flippers. Add black eyes.

14

1 Paint an oval pebble white.

2 Paint on black dots for the eyes and mouth.

3 Paint in an orange carrot nose.

Brrr! Brrr! Brrr!

1 Use a round pebble for the sunflower. Paint it a red-brown.

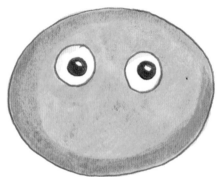

2 Now draw and paint in two eyes.

3 Add pink cheeks and a smiley face with a marker pen.

SALLY
the sunflower

4 Draw the sunflower's petal shapes onto a piece of yellow card.

5 Use scissors to carefully cut out the flower shape.

6 Stick the pebble onto the petals using PVA glue.

Bloom!

17

BARNEY
the owl

Hoot!
Hoot!

1 Paint two circles on a pebble (as shown).

2 Once dry, paint in the eyes and the beak. Leave to dry.

3 Draw and paint the wings. Add black eye pupils.

4 Add more detail to the wings.

5 Now draw and paint the feather pattern on the owl's breast.

Hoot!

Hoot!

Hoot!

6 Add his feet.

19

CACTI
spiky potted friends!

1 Paint your pebble dark green. Leave to dry.

2 Add lighter green stripes (as shown).

3 Once dry, paint small spiky clusters onto each line.

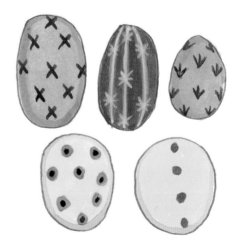

4 Fill a pot with small stones

5 Place your cacti in the pot.

6 Try making your own cactus garden using all of these designs.

CLAIRE
the chick

Cheep!

Cheep!

Cheep!

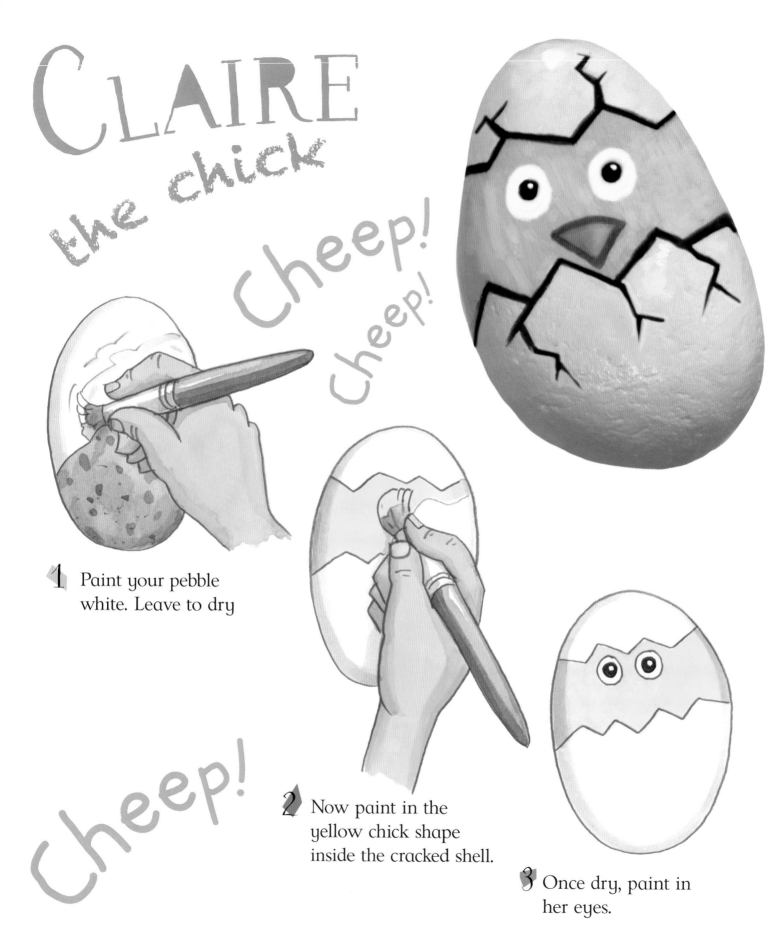

1 Paint your pebble white. Leave to dry

2 Now paint in the yellow chick shape inside the cracked shell.

3 Once dry, paint in her eyes.

22

4 Draw and paint her orange triangle beak.

5 Use black for the eggshell cracks.

Cheep!

Cheep!

Cheep!

Cheep!

Cheep!

23

TERRY the turtle

1 Carefully choose the right pebble shapes for the body, head, flippers and tail. Paint them white. Leave to dry.

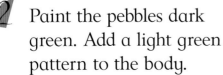 Paint the pebbles dark green. Add a light green pattern to the body.

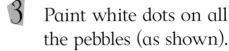 Paint white dots on all the pebbles (as shown).

4 Using a marker pen draw in the turtle's eyes and mouth.

5 Stick the pebble turtle to a piece of blue card using PVA glue.

Splash!

Splash!

Splash!

25

SAM & KATE
the ballerinas

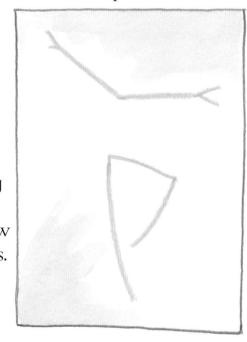

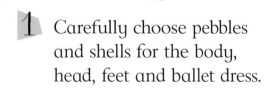

1 Carefully choose pebbles and shells for the body, head, feet and ballet dress.

2 Paint everything blue except the head. Paint the head pink.

3 Draw and paint in the hair and facial features.

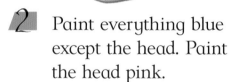

4 Place everything on a piece of paper. Now draw in arms and legs.

26

5 Now position each pebble and shell in place. Glue on using PVA.

Swish!

Twirl!

6 Repeat to stick the next ballerina in place.

Swish!

27

DANNY
the
dragonfly

Buzz!

1 Carefully choose the right shaped shells and pebbles. Now paint them white. Leave to dry.

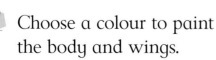

2 Choose a colour to paint the body and wings.

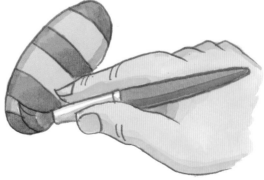

3 Paint the body pattern.

4 Draw and paint in the dragonfly's eyes and mouth.

5 Using PVA glue, stick each section onto a piece of paper to complete your dragonfly.

Buzz!

Buzz!

Buzz!

CRAZY FACES!

Have fun making some crazy faces by just using cut out paper shapes with pebbles placed on top (as shown).

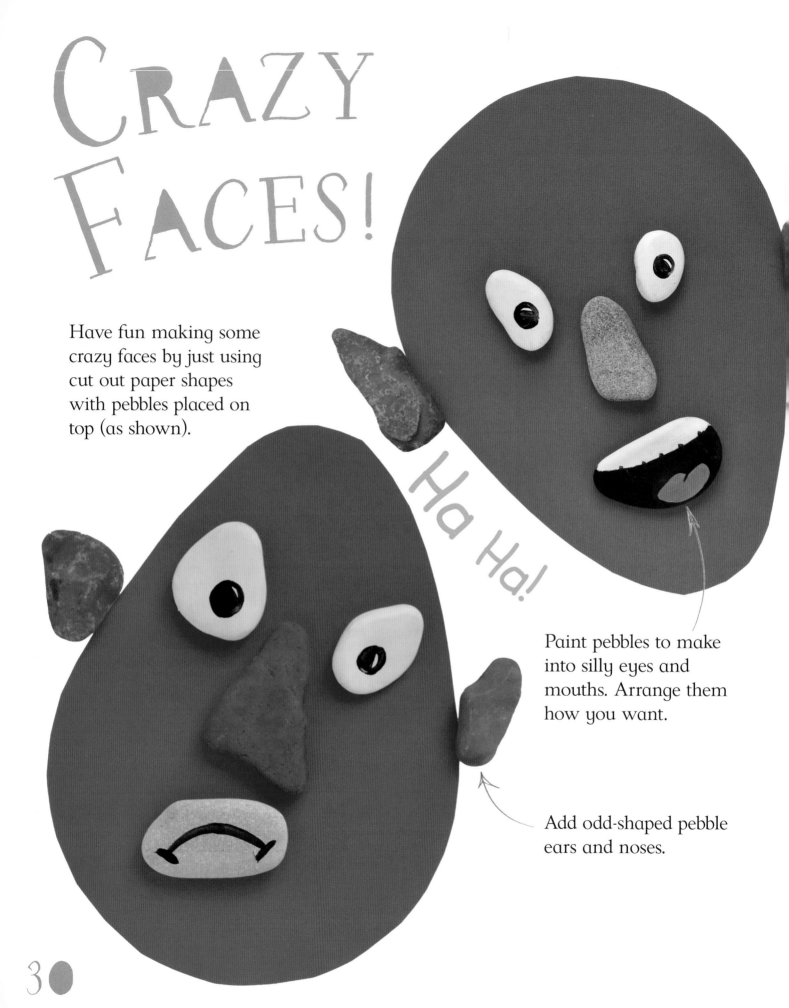

Ha Ha!

Paint pebbles to make into silly eyes and mouths. Arrange them how you want.

Add odd-shaped pebble ears and noses.

Ho Ho!

Use lots of pebbles for hair. Try different hairstyles.

GET CREATIVE...
SEE HOW
MANY FACES
YOU CAN MAKE!

31

GLOSSARY

ballerina a person who performs ballet dancing.

Bandana a square or triangular piece of cloth tied around the head to protect it or as a fashion accessory.

cactus plants with thick stems and sharp spines that grow in desert regions.

PVA glue a type of glue that is safe for use in arts and crafts activities. It can be used to stick together materials like paper and wood.

pebble a small, round, smooth stone.

scarf a long piece of cloth worn around the neck to provide warmth in cold weather or as a fashion accessory.

sunflower a type of plant, so named because its flower head looks rather like the Sun.

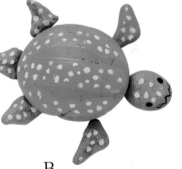

INDEX